The 12 Leadership Traps: Which One Are You Stuck In?

Marako Marcus

Published by Marako Marcus, 2024.

Copyright Page

While every precaution has been taken in the preparation of this book, the publisher assumes no responsibility for errors or omissions, or for damages resulting from the use of the information contained herein. No part of this book may be reproduced, stored in a retrieval system, or transmitted in any form or by any means, electronic, mechanical, photocopying, recording, or otherwise, without the prior written permission of the publisher, except as permitted by applicable copyright law. The information and views expressed in this book are those of the author and do not necessarily reflect the views of any organization or entity. All names, characters, and incidents in this book are fictitious. Any resemblance to real persons, living or dead, is purely coincidental.

The 12 Leadership Traps: Which One Are You Stuck In?

First Edition, December 23, 2024.

Copyright © 2024 Marako Marcus.

Written by Marako Marcus.

Introduction: The Hidden Pitfalls of Leadership

Let's face it: leadership is hard. If it were easy, everyone would do it, and we wouldn't need "leadership training" courses. But here you are—probably because you've been promoted to the role of manager or leader, and now, like most people, you're realizing you have no idea what you're doing. Don't worry, you're not alone. There are thousands of so-called "leaders" out there who are just as clueless as you. They're just better at hiding it.

Welcome to The 12 Leadership Traps, where we expose the ugliest, most embarrassing leadership behaviors that are sabotaging your career and your team's morale. And guess what? You're probably in at least one of them. Don't panic. There's hope—if you're willing to admit the truth about yourself and, more importantly, do something about it.

Why is it that some managers thrive, while others flounder and fall flat on their faces? It's simple: leadership isn't about knowing all the answers; it's about knowing when to admit you don't have them. But here's the kicker—most leaders don't do that. Instead, they fall into one of these traps, and guess what? They stay there. They become so comfortable in these traps that they start thinking they *deserve* to be there. It's like living in a moldy basement and convincing yourself it's a cozy home. Nice, right?

Let's break it down. Leadership traps aren't just funny quirks or little hiccups in your management style. No, they are major roadblocks that prevent you from being an effective leader. They make your team resent you, discredit your authority, and—this is the real kicker—slowly erode any trust they might have had in you. They make your organization spin its wheels while you're sitting there, thinking, "Why isn't anyone listening to me?" Spoiler alert: It's because you're stuck in one of these traps, and you're too oblivious to realize it.

Here's the thing: These traps don't just happen overnight. You don't wake up one morning and decide, "Hey, today I'm going to become a Control Freak or a Ghost Boss." No. It's a slow, painful descent into mediocrity. It starts innocently enough—maybe you're a little too overbearing, or maybe you like to keep tabs on everyone's performance. Next thing you know, you've morphed into the Spreadsheet Overlord or the Cheerleader, tossing out compliments like candy, all the while avoiding tough feedback like the plague. And guess what? It's already too late. You've become the problem, and your team knows it.

You'll probably read this book thinking, "I'm not like that. I'm fine. It's everyone else who's the issue." Right. That's how we all start. It's called denial. But guess what? If you're in a leadership position, you're the one accountable for the success or failure of your team. And if your team isn't doing well, you can bet your bottom dollar it's because you've slipped into one of these traps. Maybe not all of them, but certainly one or two. The Ghost Boss doesn't get to complain when their team isn't pulling their weight. The Volcano leader doesn't get to throw tantrums and then wonder why no one wants to work with them. The Zen Master doesn't get to be aloof and expect results to magically happen. News flash: leadership takes work, self-awareness, and the ability to look in the mirror and say, "Yeah, I'm probably doing this all wrong."

In this book, we're going to look at The 12 Leadership Traps in all their glorious forms. You'll recognize them, not because you're brilliant, but because you've fallen into one of them at some point in your career. Trust me. You have. And that's okay. The first step to fixing it is recognizing that you're stuck. In the coming chapters, you'll see these traps for what they are: self-inflicted wounds on your leadership reputation, all wrapped up in a nice little bow of denial.

THE 12 LEADERSHIP TRAPS: WHICH ONE ARE YOU STUCK IN?

But don't worry—this isn't just about pointing out your flaws (though, let's be honest, that's a big part of it). This is also about breaking free. Because here's the truth: you can break free from these traps. It's not rocket science. In fact, most of it boils down to simple things you're already capable of—like listening, delegating, being present, and having hard conversations. But if you don't recognize the trap you're in, how are you ever going to get out?

This book isn't here to coddle you. It's not a "rah-rah, you're amazing" kind of read. It's blunt, it's dry, and it will make you squirm in your seat because you'll probably realize that you are the problem. But that's the first step in becoming a better leader: owning your mistakes and working to correct them. No one is born a perfect leader, and there's no magic formula to fix it overnight. But with a little effort, a dash of humility, and a lot of self-reflection, you can stop being the leader your team dreads—and start being the leader they actually respect.

Ready to face the truth? Good. Let's dive in.

Self-Assessment: Are You Stuck in a Leadership Trap?

In this chapter, you'll find a series of 48 self-assessment questions that will help you identify whether you're stuck in any of the 12 leadership traps we've covered. Each trait is broken down into four questions, each beginning with "To what extent." For each statement, rate yourself on a scale of 1 to 5, where:

1 = Almost Never
2 = Rarely
3 = Sometimes
4 = Frequently
5 = Almost Always

The goal is to be brutally honest with yourself. No one's going to see these answers except you. If you find yourself answering with a 4 or 5 in multiple areas, you might be stuck in a trap. Don't worry. We'll get you out.

The Control Freak (Micromanager)

1. To what extent do I feel uncomfortable delegating tasks to my team and prefer to do things myself?
2. To what extent do I check in on my team frequently, even when they haven't asked for help or guidance?
3. To what extent do I believe that no one can do a task as well as I can?
4. To what extent do I find myself getting frustrated when my team doesn't follow my exact instructions or processes?

THE 12 LEADERSHIP TRAPS: WHICH ONE ARE YOU STUCK IN?

The Ghost Boss (Absent Leader)

1. To what extent do I find myself disengaged in day-to-day team operations and prefer to let others handle issues without my involvement?
2. To what extent do I avoid giving clear direction or feedback, leaving my team to figure things out on their own?
3. To what extent do I fail to check in on my team's well-being or progress?
4. To what extent do I let important decisions be made by others without offering my input or guidance?

The Cheerleader (Unrealistic Optimist)

1. To what extent do I focus on giving positive feedback, even when performance or outcomes don't warrant it?
2. To what extent do I avoid difficult conversations about poor performance or missed targets, preferring to keep morale high?
3. To what extent do I try to motivate my team with endless encouragement but fail to provide constructive criticism?
4. To what extent do I believe that being overly positive will keep the team motivated, regardless of real issues?

The Volcano (Passionate Explosive)

1. To what extent do I find myself displaying emotions when something goes wrong?
2. To what extent do I react emotionally to stress, even when it affects the team or the situation?
3. To what extent do I let my frustration show in front of my team, making them feel anxious or fearful?
4. To what extent do I escalate conflicts unnecessarily, making small problems seem bigger than they are?

The Visionary (Big Ideas, No Execution)

1. To what extent do I constantly come up with new ideas but fail to follow through on them?
2. To what extent do I find myself getting lost in the excitement of the "big picture" and neglecting the practical steps to achieve it?
3. To what extent do I expect my team to execute on ideas that I haven't fully developed or planned?
4. To what extent do I focus more on talking about future goals than on the day-to-day actions needed to achieve them?

The Spreadsheet Overlord (Obsessed with Data)

1. To what extent do I focus more on tracking metrics, reports, and numbers than on understanding the people behind the work?
2. To what extent do I prioritize data over employee input, creativity, and feedback in decision-making?
3. To what extent do I believe that performance can be accurately measured and controlled solely through data and numbers?
4. To what extent do I find myself dismissing people's ideas or concerns if they don't align with the numbers?

The Social Butterfly (Office Politician)

1. To what extent do I focus on building personal relationships at the expense of my team's productivity or well-being?
2. To what extent do I spend more time engaging in office gossip or politics than on actual work-related discussions?
3. To what extent do I prioritize being liked over making tough but necessary decisions?
4. To what extent do I try to influence others to maintain my

THE 12 LEADERSHIP TRAPS: WHICH ONE ARE YOU STUCK IN?

social standing or image in the workplace?

The Rulebook (Rigid and Inflexible)

1. To what extent do I believe that rules and procedures should always be followed, regardless of context or circumstances?
2. To what extent do I find it difficult to adapt or change plans when the situation requires flexibility?
3. To what extent do I prioritize rules over people, even when breaking them could lead to a better outcome?
4. To what extent do I find myself unwilling to make exceptions or find creative solutions outside of established guidelines?

The Idea Tornado (Non-Stop New Ideas)

1. To what extent do I constantly come up with new ideas but abandon them before fully implementing them?
2. To what extent do I generate so many ideas that it overwhelms my team and leads to unfinished projects?
3. To what extent do I expect my team to follow through on ideas that I've just come up with without proper planning or prioritization?
4. To what extent do I jump from one idea to another, leaving a trail of uncompleted work behind me?

The Zen Master (Detached and Passive)

1. To what extent do I remain calm or detached, even when urgency or action is needed?
2. To what extent do I avoid conflict or difficult situations, preferring peace over addressing the real issues?
3. To what extent do I fail to inspire or motivate my team, opting instead to stay neutral and uninvolved?

4. To what extent do I ignore or overlook performance issues because I don't want to rock the boat?

The Insomniac (Overworked and Expecting the Same from Others)

1. To what extent do I overwork and expect my team to match my level of commitment and hours?
2. To what extent do I feel frustrated when my team doesn't keep up with my pace or work ethic?
3. To what extent do I push myself to the point of burnout, thinking that the team should follow my example?
4. To what extent do I fail to recognize when my own stress or exhaustion affects my team's performance?

The Diva (Self-Centered and Drama-Obsessed)

1. To what extent do I crave attention and validation from others, especially in front of my team?
2. To what extent do I make situations about me, even when they involve my team's work or issues?
3. To what extent do I stir drama or create conflict for personal gain or visibility?
4. To what extent do I prioritize my own image or ego over the well-being and success of my team?

Final Scoring

Add up your scores for each set of four questions in each leadership trap.

- 10 points and lower: You might have a small tendency toward this trait, but it's not holding you back.
- 11-15 points: This trait is definitely showing up in your leadership. Time to take action and address it.

THE 12 LEADERSHIP TRAPS: WHICH ONE ARE YOU STUCK IN?

- 16-20 points: This is your big leadership trap. It's high time to get real and make some serious changes.

Take a look at the traits where your score is high, and get ready for the hard work ahead. We'll break free from these traps—together.

Chapter 1: The Control Freak

The Control Freak. You know the type. The leader who insists on overseeing every little detail, micromanages their team's every move, and believes that nobody can do anything right without their approval. You might be sitting there reading this, thinking, "That's not me. I'm just detail-oriented." Let me stop you right there. No, you're not. You're a Control Freak. And if you're being honest with yourself, you already know it.

Let me paint you a picture. Your team has a project, and instead of stepping back, delegating, and trusting your team members to do what they're good at, you hover over them like a helicopter parent at a daycare. You check in every five minutes. You question their decisions. You insist on approving every email, every spreadsheet, every presentation. Why? Because you believe—no, you *know*—that if you don't, everything will fall apart. Everyone will mess it up, and the sky will fall. Well, guess what? You're wrong. The sky won't fall. And your team is probably miserable.

Now, let's be clear: nobody's saying that you should be hands-off to the point of being negligent. Of course, you need to provide guidance and support. But there's a fine line between being involved and being a control freak. And if you're constantly checking up on every little thing, you're crossing that line. You're making your team feel like they can't do anything without you, and that's a problem. Here's why.

WHY IT'S BAD FOR YOU and Your Team

If you've ever been micromanaged (or if you are micromanaging), you'll know the frustration. It feels like you're suffocating. You feel like your independence is stripped away, like you're just a cog in the machine. When you're the Control Freak, your team will start to feel the same way. They'll start checking out. They'll stop taking initiative. They'll get used to the idea that you don't trust them to do the job without your constant oversight.

And you know what? It's a vicious cycle. The more you hover, the more you create a sense of dependence. Your team starts waiting for your approval on everything, becoming passive, and losing the very creativity and innovation they brought to the table when they were hired. You'll start thinking, "See? I told you they couldn't handle it," but you're the one who's smothering them. You're turning them into robots who can't think for themselves.

You might say, "But I *need* to ensure quality!" Of course, you do. But there's a thing called trusting your team to do what they were hired to do. Your job is not to be the person who checks every box; your job is to set the direction, communicate the goals, and remove obstacles. If you can't let go, you're not leading; you're controlling. And control doesn't inspire respect or loyalty. It breeds resentment and disengagement.

THE ROOT OF THE PROBLEM

So why do you do it? Why do you feel the need to micromanage every single detail? It's simple: control is comforting. When you control everything, you feel safe. You think you're eliminating the possibility of failure by hovering over every task. But what you're really doing is stunting growth—your own and your team's. You're not allowing anyone to take risks, to make mistakes, or to learn. And without those opportunities, there's no room for growth.

Control freaks are often perfectionists, and perfectionism comes with a heavy price. You're afraid of making mistakes because you've convinced yourself that mistakes equal failure. You'd rather handle everything yourself than risk the outcome being less than perfect. And let's be real—perfectionism is exhausting. It's a full-time job just trying to keep everything under control. It's stressful, and frankly, it's a huge waste of time. You're probably spending hours micromanaging your team instead of focusing on the bigger picture—like, you know, leading.

HOW TO BREAK FREE FROM the Control Trap

Here's the million-dollar question: How do you break out of the Control Freak trap? The first step is simple: admit that you have a problem. You're not perfect. Your team isn't perfect. And guess what? That's okay. You need to learn to let go.

Start by setting clear expectations. Communicate what you want, and then step back. Give your team the space to execute. And here's the kicker: when they fail, don't swoop in to save them. Let them fail. Let them learn from it. Yes, it's painful. But it's the only way they're going to grow. And when they succeed, give them credit. Not everything needs to come back to you.

Next, start delegating properly. Delegate with intention. When you pass off tasks, don't just say, "Here, you do this." Take the time to explain the goal, give context, and then trust your team to get it done. If you constantly feel the need to micromanage, ask yourself: Is this something that only I can do? Is this task essential to the success of the project? If the answer is no, then stop hovering.

And finally, check your ego. Letting go of control is a humbling experience. It forces you to admit that your team can handle things without you. Your job is to empower, not to oversee. Let your team take ownership. You'll be amazed at how quickly they rise to the challenge when you stop trying to control every little detail.

FINAL THOUGHTS

Being a Control Freak isn't just annoying for your team—it's a career killer for you. You're not a leader if you can't trust your team to do their job. You're just an overworked micromanager. So stop. Take a breath. Step back. And let your team do their thing. You might be surprised at how much more effective you become when you stop trying to do it all.

You're welcome.

Chapter 2: The Ghost Boss

Ah, the Ghost Boss. The leader who's there in body but absent in every other way. You've seen them: they show up to work, maybe even for the daily meeting, but mentally, emotionally, and physically—they might as well be on vacation. They're so disconnected from the team that the only time they make an appearance is when it's too late, and by then, the damage is done. If this sounds like you, don't worry, we're about to get real about it. Buckle up.

Let me ask you something: how many times have you shown up to a meeting with your team, only to zone out and think about what you'll be having for lunch? Or better yet, how many times have you just let your team handle everything because it's easier to *not* be involved? We've all been there. But as a leader, this is where you're making a huge mistake. You can't lead from the sidelines. If you're not actively engaged, you're not leading at all. And guess what? Your team knows it. They see you as a figurehead at best, and an absentee leader at worst.

WHY IT'S BAD FOR YOU and Your Team

Here's the thing about being a Ghost Boss: it's not just about showing up to work physically. It's about showing up in a meaningful way. When you fail to engage with your team, when you're emotionally checked out, it sends a message loud and clear: *I don't care.* And your team? They'll start to feel the same way. They'll stop seeking your guidance because, frankly, they've learned not to expect it. They'll stop bringing up new ideas because, why bother? You're not listening anyway. Over time, they'll lose their drive, their passion, and their respect for you. And what happens when that happens? You'll find yourself in the position of having to *repair* relationships and rebuild trust, which—let's be honest—takes a lot more effort than just showing up in the first place.

And let's talk about the impact on performance. If you're not engaged with the day-to-day operations, how do you know what's really going on? Are you aware of the team dynamics? Are you aware of how projects are progressing, or—better yet—regressing? When you're physically or emotionally absent, you're creating an environment where your team is left to their own devices. They'll do their best, but without your leadership, it's like trying to navigate through a storm with no compass. If you're not steering the ship, it's just a matter of time before the crew runs aground.

THE ROOT OF THE PROBLEM

So why does this happen? Why do you, the leader, turn into a Ghost Boss? It's simple, really: you're too busy. You've got too many other things on your plate. You're running from meeting to meeting, answering emails, putting out fires, and then—boom—you find yourself in a meeting with your team, but your mind is somewhere else. Maybe you're thinking about that client you need to call, or the report that's overdue. You're so swamped with tasks that you forget to lead. But here's the cold truth: If you're not leading, then what the hell are you doing?

You might think that by stepping back, you're giving your team space to take ownership, and while that's true to an extent, you can't just ghost them and assume everything will magically get done. Leadership doesn't work that way. You have to be present—not just physically, but mentally and emotionally as well. Otherwise, your team will feel abandoned, and that's when the real problems begin.

Another issue? Avoidance. If you're a Ghost Boss, chances are you're avoiding the tough conversations. Whether it's addressing performance issues, conflict within the team, or giving feedback—anything that's uncomfortable, you dodge. It's easier to pretend the problem doesn't exist. But let me tell you: it's not going away. And when you don't address it, your team loses faith in your ability to lead them through the tough stuff. Avoidance might feel comfortable for a while, but it's a ticking time bomb.

HOW TO BREAK FREE FROM the Ghost Trap

Now, you're probably wondering, "Okay, I get it. I'm a Ghost Boss. So what now?" It's time to step up, start showing up, and take responsibility for being the leader your team needs. Let's start with the basics. Engage with your team. I don't mean just walking by their desks and saying "Hi" like you've checked the box for being 'present.' I mean actually talk to them. Have conversations. Ask about their progress. Ask about their challenges. Get to know what's going on in their world. It's not enough to just pop in for status updates. You need to show genuine interest in their work, in their development, and in their success.

Next, schedule regular check-ins. And not the kind of check-ins where you just say, "Is everything okay?" followed by a list of tasks you want completed. No. This is about creating a space for open dialogue. This is your opportunity to coach, to mentor, and to get a pulse on what's really happening. If you're not having these conversations, then you're not really leading. Period.

Also, you need to lean into discomfort. Address the hard stuff. The conflicts, the underperformance, the issues that you'd rather pretend don't exist. If you want to be a true leader, you've got to be willing to have the uncomfortable conversations. Put down the email, walk into the room, and face the issue head-on. Avoiding it only makes it worse, and your team will respect you more for addressing it than they will for ignoring it.

And finally, be consistent. Don't just show up for a day or a week and then disappear again. Leadership requires consistency. Your team needs to know that they can count on you to be present—physically, mentally, and emotionally. This isn't about being perfect. It's about being reliable and engaged. Show your team that you're in this with them, day in and day out.

FINAL THOUGHTS

Being a Ghost Boss isn't just about being absent physically—it's about being absent in every other way. If you're not present, your team won't know what direction to take. You're leaving them in the dark. So, take a deep breath, step out from behind your email, and start leading. Show up. Be there. Engage. Your team will thank you, and you'll start seeing real results—if you're brave enough to take the first step.

Now go on, stop being a ghost.

Chapter 3: The Cheerleader

Here's the thing: being a cheerleader is great... if you're at a high school pep rally. But in the boardroom, it's not so effective. The Cheerleader Boss—the one who's always there, clapping their hands and saying, "Great job, team!"—sounds great on paper, but here's the kicker: they're doing more harm than good. If you're stuck in this leadership trap, don't worry, I'm here to tell you why that "rah-rah" attitude is holding you back from being the leader you think you are.

Let's start with the basics: positive reinforcement is important. Yes, you read that right. Everyone likes to feel appreciated and recognized. But there's a huge difference between encouraging your team and blindly praising them without any real substance. If you're the leader who's constantly handing out participation trophies and telling everyone how amazing they are, even when they've just delivered subpar results, you're not leading—you're enabling. And enabling doesn't build great teams. It builds teams that think mediocrity is good enough. So, if you're stuck in the Cheerleader Trap, it's time to rethink how you offer support.

THE PROBLEM WITH OVER-Optimism

Now, let's talk about optimism. Optimism is wonderful, but too much of it can become toxic. You're that boss who walks into a room full of problems and thinks, "It'll be fine, everyone! We've got this!" while your team internally rolls their eyes. Sure, they might nod and smile, but deep down, they know things aren't fine. You're so hell-bent on making everything sound great that you ignore the obvious issues that need to be addressed. This is the part where your enthusiasm is more about avoiding the uncomfortable than actually confronting the reality of the situation. The truth? You're creating an environment where no one feels safe enough to raise their hand and say, "Hey, I'm struggling here."

Let's be clear—constant positivity and blind encouragement don't drive results. They cover up problems and make it hard for your team to have real, tough conversations. They need solutions, not pep talks. Your team doesn't need a cheerleader, they need a leader who will help them navigate through obstacles, not someone who slaps a smile on everything and pretends that everything's okay.

THE ACCOUNTABILITY Gap

Here's where the Cheerleader really stumbles: accountability. If you're busy pumping everyone up with a constant stream of high-fives and empty "You're doing great!" statements, you're completely avoiding one of your most crucial responsibilities as a leader: holding people accountable. Accountability isn't about nitpicking every little detail—it's about ensuring that the work gets done, the standards are met, and the results align with the team's goals.

When you're the type of leader who only offers praise but never follows up with action, you're not helping your team succeed. You're letting them flounder. Without accountability, people don't know where they stand. They have no idea whether they're actually performing well or just skating by on empty praise. And this is where the wheels start to fall off. Teams that aren't held accountable stop pushing for excellence. They'll do the bare minimum and coast, waiting for the next round of fake praise. That's not leadership, it's babysitting.

WHY YOU'RE DODGING the Hard Conversations

If you're stuck in the Cheerleader Trap, chances are you're avoiding the tough conversations. You're so focused on keeping the mood light and positive that you're dodging performance reviews, feedback sessions, and uncomfortable truths. The problem with this is simple: you're not doing anyone any favors. If you don't address the issues head-on, they fester, and your team ends up just going through the motions. They don't feel challenged, they don't feel inspired, and they don't improve. Your team doesn't need another pat on the back. They need a challenge, a clear path to improvement, and a leader who will confront the issues directly, even when it's uncomfortable.

If you're serious about leading, stop running from difficult conversations. Start holding people accountable for the work they're doing, even if it means giving constructive feedback that isn't all rainbows and butterflies. It's not about being harsh; it's about being honest and helping your team get better.

HOW TO GET OUT OF THE Cheerleader Trap

So, how do you break free from this cycle of empty praise and avoidance? It's actually not that hard—start being real. You don't need to tear your team apart with harsh criticism, but you do need to stop pretending that everything is perfect when it's not. Here's what you can do:

First, provide constructive feedback. Praise is easy, but real feedback that helps people grow? That takes guts. Give praise when it's earned, but don't be afraid to point out where things could improve. People respect a leader who's willing to be honest, even when it's uncomfortable. Be specific about what went well and what didn't. Don't sugarcoat it. This is how you set clear expectations.

Second, start setting clear standards and expectations. Make sure your team knows exactly what success looks like and hold them to it. If someone's falling short, it's not enough to just cheer them on and hope they do better. You need to have a conversation about why they're falling short and what needs to change. Accountability isn't about being a jerk—it's about setting your team up for success.

Third, embrace the tough conversations. If you don't want to end up as the boss who's seen as a pushover, you have to stop avoiding conflict. Whether it's performance issues or interpersonal conflicts, address them head-on. Your team will respect you more for it, and they'll trust that you're invested in their success.

FINAL THOUGHTS

At the end of the day, the Cheerleader Trap is a quick way to derail your leadership effectiveness. Sure, you might have a team that likes you, but are they succeeding? Are they improving? Probably not. If you want to actually lead, you need to drop the pom-poms and start having the tough conversations. Be honest, set clear expectations, and hold your team accountable. Only then will you truly lead them to greatness. So, stop with the "You got this!" and start leading like you mean it.

Chapter 4: The Volcano

Ah, the Volcano Leader. If you're stuck in this trap, there's no mistaking it—you've left a trail of singed employees, uncomfortable silences, and team members who now communicate in hushed tones behind your back. The Volcano is the boss who explodes without warning. They're the ones whose temper flares up over the smallest misstep, turning even minor issues into full-blown eruptions. A little flare-up here and there is normal, but if you're consistently lobbing verbal grenades at your team, you're not a leader, you're a walking HR complaint.

You've probably convinced yourself that your outbursts show authority or demonstrate how passionate you are about getting things done. Let me burst your bubble: that's a delusion. Sure, your team might jump into action after a fiery eruption, but it's out of fear, not respect. They're not getting more productive; they're just trying to avoid becoming the next target of your wrath. Congratulations, you've created an environment where no one dares to speak up. But hey, if making people walk on eggshells is your idea of leadership, keep doing what you're doing.

THE PROBLEM WITH VOLCANIC Leadership

Let's break down the problem here. When you're the Volcano Leader, everything becomes a crisis. Every mistake, every missed deadline, every little hiccup in the workflow leads to an explosion of frustration. Do you honestly think that's effective? The thing is, people don't work better under pressure like this. They just get anxious. They tiptoe around you, trying not to make waves, because the last thing they want is to trigger another eruption. Here's the reality: your team won't be *more* productive because they're scared of you; they'll be less engaged, less creative, and more likely to look for a way out.

Now, you might argue that your explosions are justified because the stakes are high, and things need to be done right. Fair enough, but if every little bump in the road sets you off, you've got a serious problem. No one wants to be around a boss who has the emotional control of a toddler denied a snack. If you're always in crisis mode, your team will quickly burn out from the emotional whiplash. They can't predict when the next eruption will happen, and they certainly don't know how to deal with it.

So, what's the solution here? Control your emotions. You don't need to scream, stare, or start throwing around accusations every time something doesn't go as planned. In fact, I'll go one further: the more you control your emotions, the more your team will respect you. It shows maturity. It shows confidence. It shows you can handle pressure without losing your mind. And guess what? You won't be the office pariah anymore. You'll actually be the leader people want to follow.

THE IMPACT ON YOUR Team

It's easy to think that your eruptions only affect you, but in reality, they're causing ripples across your entire team. When you scream, storm out of meetings, or tear people down publicly, you're undermining trust. Employees need to feel safe in their environment to speak up, share ideas, and make mistakes. They need to know that they're not walking into a minefield every time they offer feedback or ask for help. But if you're the Volcano, you're creating a culture of fear. Your team won't want to take risks. They won't want to innovate. Why? Because they don't know how you're going to react.

A leader's job isn't just to get results; it's to foster a culture where employees can thrive, take initiative, and learn from their mistakes. The Volcano leader prevents this by creating an atmosphere of constant tension. No one wants to be the person who accidentally sets off the next explosion. People will disengage, shut down, and start looking for other opportunities. They'll be mentally checked out before they even leave the office.

THE DOWNWARD SPIRAL of Fear-Based Leadership

If you keep blowing up, there's a dangerous side effect: fear-based leadership. This is a trap that's hard to escape once you've fallen into it, because you'll start thinking that your outbursts are necessary to get things done. But all you're doing is stifling communication and creativity. People will start doing just enough to get by—flying under the radar, covering their tracks, and avoiding any direct confrontation with you. Innovation? Creativity? Collaboration? Gone. You've created an atmosphere where the best ideas aren't shared because no one wants to take the risk of being called out for something that's not even their fault.

You can't build a high-performing team on fear. If your team is more focused on keeping their heads down than on doing great work, it's time to reassess how you lead. If you're operating in a constant state of emergency, what kind of example are you setting? That leadership is about crisis management and drama? Wrong. Leadership is about steady guidance, support, and, most importantly, emotional maturity.

HOW TO GET OUT OF THE Volcano Trap

So, how do you cool things down? It's simple: breathe. Seriously. Take a moment to step back before reacting. When things go wrong, take a deep breath, count to ten, and then respond with clarity, not emotion. If you feel an eruption coming on, walk away, gather your thoughts, and address the issue calmly and directly. It's about responding to situations, not reacting. When you take control of your emotions, you gain con-

THE 12 LEADERSHIP TRAPS: WHICH ONE ARE YOU STUCK IN?

trol over the situation. Your team will start to see you as a steady, reliable leader, not a ticking time bomb.

Start with building emotional intelligence. Learn to recognize when your temper is about to flare, and find ways to defuse it before it blows. This could mean stepping outside for a few minutes, journaling your thoughts, or practicing deep breathing exercises. Anything that helps you stay calm under pressure. Because, spoiler alert, the world isn't ending every time something goes wrong. And when you show your team that you can handle pressure with composure, they'll feel more confident in your leadership.

FINAL THOUGHTS

If you're a Volcano Leader, the good news is you can change. You don't have to continue burning bridges with your team. If you want to be a true leader, one who's respected and trusted, you have to keep your cool. Stop throwing tantrums every time something doesn't go according to plan. Embrace the art of calm, thoughtful leadership. Your team will thank you for it. So, cool down, take control of your emotions, and start leading with maturity and grace. No more eruptions.

Chapter 5: The Visionary

Oh, the Visionary Leader. Big ideas, lofty goals, and dreams that could fill up an entire whiteboard. You're the one who stands up in meetings, talks about "disrupting industries" and "changing the world," and everyone gets fired up—at least for the first five minutes. But here's the problem: that's all you've got. The idea is shiny and exciting, but when it comes to turning that big vision into action, you're like a deer in headlights. The Visionary Leader is great at dreaming big, but when it's time to roll up their sleeves and get to the hard work of execution, they freeze. It's all talk, no walk. Sound familiar?

Let's be clear. Having a grand vision is not the problem. Visionaries are often incredibly inspiring. They can rally the troops, paint a picture of a better future, and get people excited about a cause. But once the excitement wears off, and reality sets in, the problem becomes clear: there's no plan. The vision is still just an idea, and without a solid strategy or concrete steps, it goes nowhere. You can inspire your team all you want, but without the ability to follow through and execute, all you're doing is setting them up for disappointment.

THE PROBLEM WITH VISIONARY Leadership

Here's the thing about big ideas: they don't execute themselves. Your team doesn't need another pep talk; they need a leader who can bridge the gap between inspiration and action. If you're stuck in the Visionary trap, you're probably great at coming up with new projects, new ways to "innovate," and new ideas to shake things up. But the issue is, you're so enamored with the next shiny thing that you leave the important stuff undone. You get distracted by the possibilities, while the current initiatives fall through the cracks.

Your employees are probably nodding along, smiling, and going along with your latest bright idea, but deep down they're wondering: "When is this ever going to happen?" The Visionary Leader often thinks that just having the idea is enough. The truth? It's just the starting point. Without clear goals, milestones, and a plan to get there, your big ideas are nothing but empty promises. And if you keep doing this over and over, your credibility with your team will take a hit.

THE IMPACT ON YOUR Team

Let's talk about the damage you're doing. When you lead with nothing but vision and no action plan, you're creating a culture of unmet expectations. You've rallied your team, fired them up with your ideas, and set them off with the belief that something great is coming. But when they turn around and look for direction, they find...nothing. No plan. No roadmap. Just a vague hope that something magical will happen. It's frustrating, and frankly, it's demotivating.

The constant cycle of "let's try this new thing" without any follow-through causes employees to disengage. They'll start doubting your ability to lead because they're always left with a half-baked vision that never sees the light of day. Eventually, they'll stop getting excited about your ideas. They'll stop listening to the next great initiative you're planning, because they know it's just another empty promise. They'll wait for you to come up with something that actually works, but in the meantime, they'll get comfortable with the idea that "nothing will ever get done."

This isn't just frustrating for your team. It's downright toxic. You're wasting their time and energy by creating a revolving door of projects that never come to fruition. Your team members don't want to be led by someone who's all talk and no action. They want a leader who knows how to execute, follow through, and turn vision into reality.

THE DOWNWARD SPIRAL of Idea Fatigue

What happens when this pattern continues? Your team starts to get idea fatigue. You know, that feeling of exhaustion that sets in every time you present a new vision that sounds like the last five you presented. It's the look of "Here we go again" that appears in your team's eyes whenever you open your mouth. They're tired of hearing about the next great thing without seeing any results from the last great thing. You're killing their motivation, and with it, their ability to work toward any goal. When you constantly present new ideas without the capacity to execute, you breed apathy. And that's the last thing a team needs from a leader.

HOW TO GET OUT OF THE Visionary Trap

You're not stuck here forever. Breaking out of the Visionary trap takes a little discipline and a lot of self-awareness. First, stop selling a dream and start providing a roadmap. A big vision can be a great motivator, but it needs to be supported by action steps, deadlines, and clear roles and responsibilities. Get into the details. What exactly needs to happen for this idea to become a reality? Break the vision down into tangible goals. Assign specific tasks to people who are responsible for each step. This isn't just about having a dream. It's about building a practical plan that you can work on every day, with measurable progress.

Start by creating accountability. Hold yourself accountable for moving the vision forward, and hold your team accountable for delivering on their responsibilities. Just as you need a clear plan to follow, you need to create a system that tracks progress and keeps people on target. Give your team a reason to believe that this vision is actually going somewhere.

THE 12 LEADERSHIP TRAPS: WHICH ONE ARE YOU STUCK IN?

FINAL THOUGHTS

Being a Visionary Leader isn't a curse. In fact, it's a strength—if you're willing to pair it with execution. No one is saying you should stop dreaming. The world needs visionaries. But a vision without a plan is just a fantasy. So get your act together. You can't lead on ideas alone. If you want to be taken seriously, you need to prove you can turn your grand concepts into actionable outcomes. Otherwise, you'll keep running in circles, talking about how amazing things could be, and watching your team lose faith in you. Keep dreaming big, but remember: dreams only come true when you wake up and get to work.

Chapter 6: The Spreadsheet Overlord

Let's talk about the Spreadsheet Overlord. The one who's so obsessed with data, metrics, and KPIs that they could probably recite your company's profit margins in their sleep—yet somehow, they're unable to remember the last time they actually spoke to a real human being about what's going on in the business. This leader doesn't just love spreadsheets; they worship them. They believe that the only true measure of success is what's in those cells. Numbers are king, and anything that doesn't fit neatly into a table or a chart is irrelevant. People, creativity, intuition—those things don't matter. As long as the numbers are good, everything else can be ignored.

Don't get me wrong. Metrics are important. Data drives decisions, and tracking performance is crucial for any business. But here's where the Spreadsheet Overlord goes wrong: they become so fixated on the numbers that they forget what the numbers actually represent. They lose sight of the fact that behind every metric, behind every data point, is a human being. And those humans? They don't run on formulas or spreadsheets. They run on motivation, creativity, trust, and collaboration. So, while you're pouring over Excel, analyzing profit margins to the decimal point, your team is getting demotivated, disengaged, and burned out.

THE PROBLEM WITH SPREADSHEET Overlord Leadership

It's all about balance. The Spreadsheet Overlord can't seem to grasp this. They think that if they just dig a little deeper into the numbers, they'll uncover the magic formula for success. But the more time they spend in the weeds of data, the less time they spend leading their team. They get so caught up in refining their Excel skills that they forget the true value of leadership: people.

When you prioritize data over people, you're missing the point. You're so busy looking at the numbers that you forget to check in with your team and see how they're feeling, what they're struggling with, or whether they even understand the metrics you're so obsessed with. You're creating a disconnect. Your team is looking at you like you're speaking a foreign language. They can't relate to all those figures and percentages you're spouting. They just want to know how to do their job well, how to work together effectively, and how to achieve goals that make sense in the real world, not just in your data dashboard.

THE IMPACT ON YOUR Team

If you're a Spreadsheet Overlord, here's the impact you're having on your team: they're not engaged. They don't feel heard or seen. Why? Because you're too busy looking at charts to understand what's really going on. The constant focus on numbers leads to a lack of connection, which erodes trust. Your team is working their tails off, but all they hear from you are more spreadsheets, more numbers, more metrics. There's no conversation about their personal development, their struggles, or how they feel about the work they're doing. And worse, you're probably evaluating their performance based solely on numbers, without considering the context or the human element involved.

When leaders become Spreadsheet Overlords, they start making decisions based on numbers alone. Sure, the metrics might be great, but what happens when those numbers don't tell the whole story? What happens when a team member is struggling but their performance is still looking good on paper? What happens when a team is going above and beyond, but the data doesn't reflect their hard work because they've been working on less measurable, but equally important, tasks? These are questions the Spreadsheet Overlord doesn't ask. Instead, they just point to the chart and say, "See? We're doing great!" But that's only true if you completely ignore the human side of the equation.

HOW TO BREAK FREE FROM Spreadsheet Overlord Syndrome

Step one: acknowledge that people are not spreadsheets. They are complex, emotional, motivated individuals who sometimes do their best work when they feel heard, valued, and appreciated. So, start looking at the people behind the numbers. When you get a performance report or a data sheet, make sure you take the time to understand what's behind the numbers. Have conversations with your team. Ask them how they're feeling, what challenges they're facing, and what they need from you. Don't just look at their performance metrics—look at their performance in context.

Step two: stop obsessing over perfection. No one is going to hit every number, every target, every time. As a leader, it's your job to help your team achieve their goals—not beat them over the head with unattainable expectations. Set clear, achievable targets, but be flexible. Understand that things will change, plans will shift, and not everything can be measured in neat little boxes. The more you're willing to embrace imperfection, the more you'll create a culture where your team feels safe to take risks and experiment. And that's where real innovation happens—not in perfect numbers, but in the messy, human process of trying new things and learning from mistakes.

Step three: engage with your team. Your spreadsheets might tell you a lot about your business, but they don't tell you about the culture, the morale, or the underlying dynamics of your team. To truly lead, you need to get out of your office and spend time with your people. Walk around. Have informal conversations. Ask questions that go beyond the numbers. Get to know your team members as people, not just employees who fill in rows and columns of data. When you start focusing on them as individuals and building a culture of trust, the results will follow—metrics will improve because your team will be more engaged, more motivated, and more productive.

FINAL THOUGHTS

Being a Spreadsheet Overlord isn't inherently bad—after all, data is essential. But when it becomes your sole focus, you lose sight of what leadership is truly about: inspiring, supporting, and developing your team. If you want to break out of this trap, you need to put down the spreadsheets for a minute and pick up the phone. Have a conversation. Listen to your team. And then, maybe, you can use your data to make informed decisions about how to help them grow and succeed. Until then, all you're doing is using numbers to hide behind the hard work of actually leading.

Chapter 7: The Social Butterfly

Ah, the Social Butterfly—the leader who's more interested in being liked than actually leading. The one who is constantly floating around the office, popping into people's cubicles for chats, making small talk in the break room, and attending every happy hour like they're auditioning for "Most Popular Manager" of the year. They're beloved by all, no doubt. Everyone knows their name, they're the first to crack a joke, and they make everyone feel "seen." But there's one glaring problem: they don't lead.

Now, don't get me wrong—being personable is a good trait. People like working with someone who's approachable, friendly, and easy to talk to. But the Social Butterfly takes it a step too far. They've got their finger on the pulse of every social event, every gossip session, every office inside joke. But when it comes to actually guiding their team, making tough decisions, or holding people accountable? Crickets. The Social Butterfly is nowhere to be found. They've mastered the art of making people feel comfortable, but they've somehow missed the part where leadership actually involves driving results and making difficult calls.

THE PROBLEM WITH SOCIAL Butterfly Leadership

This kind of leadership might win you some popularity points, but it's a fast track to irrelevance in the long run. The Social Butterfly's main concern is keeping everyone happy and keeping the peace, which sounds nice in theory. But in practice, it leads to a lack of direction, weak decision-making, and a team that's not challenged to grow. As a leader, your job isn't to be everyone's best friend. It's to make tough decisions, even if they're not going to win you any popularity contests. But the Social Butterfly avoids that. Why? Because difficult decisions might alienate people, and God forbid anyone feels uncomfortable. So instead of making decisions, they let things fester, hoping it'll all blow over. Spoiler: it doesn't.

The Social Butterfly is the leader who tells everyone they're "doing great" even when they're clearly not. Why? Because it's easier to say that than to give constructive criticism or have an uncomfortable conversation. The result? People continue to underperform, knowing full well they're not being held accountable. And the Social Butterfly? They're still floating around, keeping the peace, avoiding confrontation, and pretending everything is fine. But deep down, they know they're not actually leading anyone—they're just being liked.

THE IMPACT ON YOUR Team

When you're a Social Butterfly, your team doesn't respect you—they just like you. And there's a huge difference. Respect is earned through leadership, accountability, and the ability to make hard decisions. Being liked is a byproduct of being a competent leader, but it's not the goal. If your team only likes you, they won't follow you when things get tough. They'll start to question your ability to lead when you can't make the tough calls or when they realize you've been avoiding hard conversations because you don't want to rock the boat.

The Social Butterfly's lack of accountability also breeds complacency. If your team knows that you'll never give them honest feedback or hold them to a high standard, they'll stop trying to improve. Why should they? As long as they're friends with you, they're good. But when it comes time to perform at a high level or execute on a challenging project, the lack of discipline will show. And guess what? Your team won't be ready. They won't have the mental fortitude to handle pressure because you've never held them to a standard that challenges them. Instead, they've just been getting by, enjoying the "good vibes" without ever being asked to really step up.

HOW TO BREAK FREE FROM Social Butterfly Syndrome

Step one: stop worrying about being liked. Leadership isn't about making everyone your best friend. It's about making the hard decisions and standing firm when things get difficult. Yes, you'll lose some fans along the way. People might not like you when you give them constructive feedback or when you make a decision they don't agree with. But here's the thing: they'll respect you. And respect is far more valuable than being liked. As a leader, you don't need a fan club—you need a team that's committed to the mission, that trusts you to make the tough calls, and that knows you'll hold them accountable for delivering results.

Step two: get comfortable with discomfort. The Social Butterfly avoids uncomfortable situations. They shy away from conflict, and they'd rather sweep problems under the rug than confront them head-on. But great leaders lean into discomfort. They know that avoiding hard conversations is a recipe for disaster. If someone's underperforming, you need to address it. If the team is veering off track, you need to get them back in line. It won't always be fun, but it's necessary. Start having the uncomfortable conversations. Start holding people accountable. Start setting clear expectations. And yes, it might make you unpopular for a while, but it will make you a better leader.

Step three: learn how to say no. The Social Butterfly says yes to everything because they don't want to disappoint anyone. But saying yes to everything means you're saying no to what matters. As a leader, you can't afford to be pulled in every direction by every request, every social gathering, and every opportunity for praise. You need to prioritize what's best for the team and the business. Sometimes that means saying no to a lunch with a colleague or skipping a happy hour. It's time to focus on the things that matter.

FINAL THOUGHTS

The Social Butterfly's trap is all about avoiding conflict, avoiding accountability, and, ultimately, avoiding true leadership. If you're the type of leader who's more focused on being liked than on actually leading, you're setting yourself and your team up for failure. Yes, being personable is important, but it's not the be-all and end-all. Leadership is about making tough decisions, holding people accountable, and challenging your team to grow. So if you're stuck in the Social Butterfly trap, it's time to step up, get uncomfortable, and start leading. Because being liked won't get you anywhere in the long run—but being respected will.

Chapter 8: The Rulebook

Ah, the Rulebook—the leader who treats policies, procedures, and rules like gospel. Every decision, every action, every conversation is filtered through a rigid lens of "this is how we've always done it," and "these are the rules." The Rulebook's favorite pastime? Whipping out their company's handbook, quoting policies, and making sure everyone toes the line. They love rules because rules are easy. They're predictable. They don't require critical thinking or nuance. They're simple and clear-cut. The problem? Leadership isn't about rules. Leadership is about people. And the Rulebook leader doesn't seem to get that.

Let's be honest: rules are great for some things—traffic laws, safety regulations, and, you know, maybe how not to set your office on fire. But when it comes to leading a team of diverse, complex individuals who are asked to innovate, collaborate, and problem-solve, following a rulebook to the letter doesn't cut it. Every person is different. Every situation is different. A good leader knows when to bend the rules, when to question the established processes, and when to make a judgment call based on the circumstances at hand. The Rulebook leader? They won't even consider it. To them, the rule is sacred. And that's where they get stuck.

THE PROBLEM WITH RULEBOOK Leadership

The issue with leading from a rulebook is that you treat your team like automatons—just people following orders, not thinking for themselves, not applying judgment. This approach might work in a factory or assembly line, where uniformity is key, but it doesn't work in the real world of leadership. The workplace isn't a machine. It's full of human beings with emotions, opinions, and personal experiences. People don't fit neatly into boxes, and they certainly don't thrive under a micromanaged, rule-obsessed regime.

When you lead by the rulebook, you stifle creativity. You create a team of robots who are too afraid to think outside the box, for fear of stepping out of line. They learn to follow the rules, but they don't learn to adapt, innovate, or problem-solve. If you're constantly enforcing policies and procedures without considering the bigger picture, you're preventing your team from developing the skills they need to handle complex challenges. Over time, your team will stop thinking for themselves. They'll just wait for you to tell them exactly what to do next, and they'll get frustrated if you don't. This is a recipe for stagnation.

Moreover, the Rulebook leader breeds resentment. People don't want to be treated like children. They don't want to feel like they're being constantly micromanaged or judged for every small deviation from the rules. Sure, rules are important, but they're not the entire picture. When you treat everything as black-and-white, you ignore the gray areas where true leadership lies. And you end up alienating the very people you're trying to lead.

THE IMPACT ON YOUR Team

When you're the Rulebook leader, your team becomes overly dependent on you to tell them what to do. They start to lose their autonomy. They start waiting for instructions instead of taking initiative. The problem here is that leadership requires empowerment. It's your job to set the direction, yes, but then you need to trust your team to do the work, to make decisions, and to take ownership of their roles. When you're always imposing rules, you rob your team of that autonomy. You turn them into followers instead of leaders in their own right.

At the same time, the team's morale will suffer. If they feel like they're constantly walking on eggshells, scared of breaking some rule, they won't feel safe to experiment or make mistakes. And guess what? Mistakes are necessary for growth. When you only focus on enforcing the rules, you prevent your team from learning through trial and error. You create a culture of fear, not innovation. People won't take risks. They'll play it safe. And that's a surefire way to kill progress.

The Rulebook leader also tends to micromanage. Because everything is "by the book," they feel the need to monitor every little detail, ensuring that each action aligns with the prescribed rules. They get caught up in the minutiae, forgetting that leadership is about big picture thinking. In doing so, they're not only frustrating their team—they're wasting time that could be spent on more strategic, impactful work.

HOW TO BREAK FREE FROM the Rulebook Trap

Step one: learn to question the rules. Yes, rules are important, but so is judgment. The first step in breaking free from the Rulebook trap is learning when to bend the rules. Ask yourself: "Is this rule really necessary in this situation? Is it serving the greater good, or is it just an arbitrary line in the sand?" A great leader knows when to follow the rules and when to make exceptions based on context.

Step two: empower your team to make decisions. You hired these people for a reason, right? Trust them. Stop micromanaging and start giving them the freedom to think for themselves. Let them take ownership of their work and make decisions. Provide guidance when necessary, but allow your team to chart their own course. When you stop hovering over them, you'll see that they'll rise to the occasion. And when they feel empowered to make decisions, they'll develop the skills needed to handle future challenges.

Step three: embrace flexibility. Leadership requires a flexible mindset. You can't be so rigid that you're unable to adapt to changing circumstances. Life isn't black and white, and neither is leadership. Sometimes, the rules need to be broken to achieve the best results. Be willing to adjust when needed. After all, a leader who isn't flexible is one who's destined to fail in the face of change.

FINAL THOUGHTS

The Rulebook leader is a leader who is trapped by their own need for control and order. They rely too heavily on policies and procedures, forgetting that leadership is about people and judgment. If you're stuck in the Rulebook trap, it's time to loosen up. It's time to empower your team, question the rules, and be flexible. Leadership isn't about following the book to the letter; it's about using your judgment, guiding your team, and achieving results. If you're not willing to step away from the rulebook, you'll never be the leader your team needs.

Chapter 9: The Idea Tornado

Here's a special kind of leader, one who's always bursting with new ideas, a veritable whirlwind of creativity and enthusiasm. The Idea Tornado is always throwing out new concepts, strategies, and plans at a speed that can leave your head spinning. Sounds amazing, right? Well, not so fast. While an Idea Tornado might sound like the kind of leader who brings excitement to the table, the reality is far less glamorous. This leader is a master of starting things—but finishing them? Not so much.

At first, everyone in the office loves the energy and the ideas. "Wow, this leader is so creative! They've got a vision for the future! They're thinking outside the box!" And while the initial rush of new ideas is great, the problem arises when the Tornado forgets the most important part of leadership: execution. You see, it's easy to come up with big ideas. But if you don't have the ability to follow through, those ideas are just shiny distractions. They'll fizzle out before they even get off the ground.

The Idea Tornado is usually so enamored with their own ideas that they forget to follow through, leaving a trail of half-finished projects, frustrated team members, and missed opportunities. The team gets used to the idea that every few weeks there's a new shiny object to chase, but they soon learn that none of it will ever amount to anything. This creates a culture of unfulfilled potential—everyone is just waiting for the next big idea, without ever seeing anything completed.

THE PROBLEM WITH IDEA Tornado Leadership

The first problem with the Idea Tornado is their lack of focus. Every new idea comes with excitement, but there's never any clarity on which project to prioritize or what's actually worth pursuing. As a result, the team gets pulled in every direction. Projects start, but they never finish. The original idea gets lost in the shuffle, and the team is left wondering what exactly their leader is trying to achieve.

This behavior creates chaos. The tornado may create a temporary buzz, but it doesn't lead to real, meaningful outcomes. People get confused about the direction. Priorities shift so quickly that no one can keep up. The team's morale takes a hit when they realize that they're stuck in a cycle of starting something new, only to leave it incomplete as the next idea comes crashing in. Over time, they begin to disengage. It's exhausting to always feel like you're spinning in circles without seeing any tangible results.

The second problem? Lack of commitment to the process. Ideas are great, but they're just the beginning. Implementation, follow-through, and dedication to seeing something through to the end are the parts that make those ideas worthwhile. An Idea Tornado leader might spend weeks drafting plans, brainstorming sessions, and charting out big dreams—but when it comes time to do the work, they disappear into the next "great idea."

THE IMPACT ON YOUR Team

For your team, the Idea Tornado's leadership is frustrating, to say the least. They get stuck in a perpetual state of whiplash—one minute, they're focusing on one initiative, and the next, they're scrambling to start a completely new one. This leads to burnout and frustration. Team members feel like they're constantly working on a moving target, never able to gain momentum because the priorities keep shifting.

What's worse, over time, the team begins to lose faith in their leader. The constant rush of new ideas without execution signals that the leader isn't serious about making any of it work. The team starts to disengage, tuning out the leader's excitement for the next shiny object, and begin to do just enough to get by. They no longer see the point in getting too invested in the next big idea, because they know it won't stick.

HOW TO BREAK FREE FROM the Idea Tornado Trap

Step one: Commit to execution. This is where most Idea Tornado leaders fall short—they're so busy dreaming up the next big thing that they forget to commit to the current one. Pick an idea, focus on it, and give it the attention and resources it deserves. This means prioritizing projects, setting realistic timelines, and sticking with them until completion. If you're always starting something new, nothing will ever get finished.

Step two: Learn to say no. You don't have to say yes to every new idea that comes your way. As a leader, you have to be selective about what you pursue. Ask yourself: "Is this aligned with our goals? Will this help us move forward?" If the answer is no, don't waste your team's time with it. Saying no is just as important as saying yes—especially when your team is already stretched thin.

Step three: Provide clarity. When you introduce a new idea or project, be clear about what needs to be done and why it matters. Set specific goals, define success, and be transparent about the timeline and resources required. Clarity is the antidote to chaos. Without it, your team will continue to feel like they're chasing the wind.

Step four: Focus on results, not ideas. Leadership isn't about how many ideas you can generate; it's about what you can accomplish. A good leader knows that the most important thing is to get things done. If you're always spinning out new ideas, you're probably missing out on the opportunity to create real, measurable results.

FINAL THOUGHTS

The Idea Tornado is the leader who's always on the hunt for the next big thing, but never sticks around long enough to make anything happen. While new ideas are important, execution and follow-through are what matter in the end. If you're stuck in this trap, it's time to stop chasing the next shiny object and start committing to the ideas that matter. Focus, clarity, and commitment will help you break free from the tornado and become the kind of leader who gets results.

Chapter 10: The Zen Master

Ah, the Zen Master—calm, cool, and collected. You've seen them. The leader who is always at peace—so calm, so chill, they might as well have come straight from a meditation retreat in the Himalayas. On the surface, this seems like a great thing. Who wouldn't want a leader who isn't frazzled by deadlines, pressure, or conflict? But before you get carried away with the fantasy, let's pull back the curtain and take a look at the real issue here. Too much calm is a problem. In fact, if your leadership style is more "Zen Master" than "driven, decisive leader," you're in for a bumpy ride.

Let's face it: you've probably been in a meeting with a leader who responds to everything with the same serene expression and tone, whether the company is about to lose its biggest client or the team is falling behind on critical projects. "It's all good," they say, nodding thoughtfully. "Everything will work itself out." Right, sure, it's "all good." Except when it's not. And guess what? The team knows it's not all good.

The Zen Master leader has mastered the art of remaining unflappable, but that can sometimes translate into a complete lack of urgency. Your team is looking for someone who can rally them during tough times, someone who isn't just floating through the storm but is actively steering the ship. Instead, the Zen Master sits back, hands folded, content to let the storm pass. Meanwhile, projects are stalled, team morale is crumbling, and nothing gets done—except for that overwhelming sense of nothingness.

THE 12 LEADERSHIP TRAPS: WHICH ONE ARE YOU STUCK IN?

THE PROBLEM WITH THE Zen Master

The Zen Master is a master of detachment, and in leadership, detachment can quickly turn into apathy. When there's no sense of urgency, no visible reaction to crises, and no drive to push the team toward a common goal, you get a leader who's completely uninspiring. The issue is that the Zen Master's calming presence may be a comfort in certain situations, but when it comes to pushing for results, making tough decisions, and holding people accountable, their passive approach is a hindrance.

Now, don't get me wrong. There's value in staying calm under pressure—especially in highly stressful situations. But when your response to everything is "it'll all work out," your team starts to question whether you even care about the outcomes. When nothing ever seems urgent, nothing ever gets done. Teams need a leader who is passionate, driven, and who can show them that the work they're doing matters—urgency fuels motivation. If you're stuck in the Zen Master trap, you'll notice your team losing energy. They'll start questioning your commitment and, eventually, your ability to lead.

Another problem? Lack of direction. In the name of "balance," the Zen Master often avoids conflict, avoids making tough decisions, and avoids providing a clear sense of where the team should be heading. Instead of stepping up to guide, direct, and sometimes even challenge the team, the Zen Master might let things drift. The end result is that the team ends up with no clear vision or guidance, which leads to confusion and doubt.

THE IMPACT ON YOUR Team

If your team's leaders are "Zen Masters," expect to see them all sitting around, waiting for something to happen rather than making things happen. Without a sense of urgency, projects drag on. Decisions are delayed. Priorities are unclear. The team becomes stuck, unsure of where they're going or how to get there.

This lack of inspiration can be crushing. The Zen Master might be well-meaning, thinking they're maintaining a calm and positive environment for their team. But when team members are desperately looking for direction, accountability, and energy, calmness can be perceived as indifference. Your team may be waiting for someone to step up and lead them through challenges. If you're too detached from the situation, you're leaving them to figure it out on their own. And spoiler alert: they won't be able to. They're not supposed to.

The more detached the Zen Master becomes, the more disengaged the team becomes. When the team sees their leader as disconnected, they stop believing that things are going to improve, and morale tanks. It's hard to be motivated when your leader seems like they're living in a perpetual state of "meh."

HOW TO BREAK FREE FROM the Zen Master Trap

Step one: Reignite urgency. It's time to wake up and realize that leadership isn't about staying perpetually calm. When things aren't going well, show your team that you care. Demonstrate urgency. Lead by example. Show your team that you are committed to pushing through difficult times and working toward meaningful results. This doesn't mean you have to become a fire-breathing dragon every time a problem arises, but it does mean you need to take action, set priorities, and communicate a sense of purpose.

Step two: Get engaged. Leadership isn't about taking a backseat. As a leader, you have to be deeply involved in what's happening. This means engaging with your team, understanding their challenges, and offering clear direction. It's about being present and invested—not detached and passive. Step up when decisions need to be made and stop waiting for things to work themselves out. You're the one in charge, so act like it.

Step three: Instill passion and inspiration. If you're the kind of leader who's constantly detached, now's the time to reconnect with what you

THE 12 LEADERSHIP TRAPS: WHICH ONE ARE YOU STUCK IN?

care about. Passion is contagious, and if you're not passionate about the work you're leading, don't expect your team to be either. Tap into your drive, communicate your vision, and get your team excited about the work. Leadership is about motivating others to take action, not just sitting back and letting the world happen to them.

Step four: Be decisive. Stop avoiding difficult decisions and tough conversations. A Zen Master might sidestep issues in favor of "peace," but in leadership, avoidance only leads to problems down the road. Leaders need to make decisions, set direction, and hold people accountable. This is where true leadership comes into play.

FINAL THOUGHTS

Being calm and collected is a great trait in some situations, but as a leader, too much detachment can lead to disengagement and complacency. A leader who doesn't inspire action or urgency isn't leading at all—they're just waiting for things to happen. If you're stuck in the Zen Master trap, it's time to break free. Get engaged, ignite urgency, and start making things happen. The team needs you to be a leader, not just a bystander in the chaos.

Chapter 11: The Insomniac

Oh, the Insomniac. The overachiever who's always working. The one who answers emails at 2 a.m., attends every meeting, and somehow expects their team to match their endless energy and drive. They wear their exhaustion like a badge of honor, boasting about how little sleep they get and how many hours they've been logged in. "I haven't had a full night's sleep in years," they'll say with pride, as if that's some kind of accomplishment. Spoiler alert: it's not. If you're an Insomniac leader, you're probably setting a terrible example—and not just for yourself, but for your team, too.

Let's break it down. The Insomniac leader doesn't know how to shut off. Ever. They are the first to arrive in the office and the last to leave, spending more time at their desk than with their family or friends. They treat every moment of downtime as a waste of productivity. The more they work, the more they expect their team to do the same. Sound familiar? That's because it's a common trap many leaders fall into—workaholism disguised as dedication.

Now, don't get me wrong. Dedication is great. Hard work is admirable. But when you're constantly running on empty and demanding the same from everyone around you, you're only asking for trouble. Burnout. Stress. A disengaged, resentful team. All of these are on the horizon.

THE PROBLEM WITH THE Insomniac

If you're an Insomniac leader, you may think that your level of commitment to the grind is inspiring your team. You might even believe that by staying late and working weekends, you're leading by example. But here's the harsh reality: you're not inspiring anyone. In fact, you're making everyone feel like they're falling short because they can't keep up with your insane schedule. You're teaching them that work-life balance doesn't matter, that personal time is expendable, and that you expect them to sacrifice their well-being for the job.

The problem here is that the more you push yourself and your team to work harder, the more you normalize unhealthy behavior. Your team might start to feel pressured to work extra hours just to meet your expectations. They'll start to burn out. They'll resent you for it. And worst of all, they won't be as productive as they could be if you all just learned how to take a break. But you wouldn't know that, because you're too busy pushing yourself to the limit.

If you're an Insomniac, your ability to make rational decisions and think strategically will inevitably suffer. Fatigue clouds judgment. You can't possibly make sound decisions when you haven't had a good night's sleep in weeks. You're going to miss details. You're going to overlook problems. And you'll probably make a lot of mistakes along the way, which means you'll end up spending even more time trying to fix what's broken. It's a vicious cycle.

Here's another kicker: the lack of boundaries. When you're the leader, you set the tone for the team. If you never take a break, why should they? If you respond to emails at 11 p.m., guess what—they're going to think it's normal to do the same. And before long, your team is living in a perpetual state of exhaustion. You'll have an entire team running on fumes, but instead of acknowledging the problem, the Insomniac leader simply pushes harder, thinking more work will solve everything.

THE IMPACT ON YOUR Team

Here's the ugly truth: when you're an Insomniac, you're not creating a culture of hard work—you're creating a culture of burnout. Your team will start resenting you. They'll feel like they can never catch a break. And most importantly, they'll disengage. Disengagement is the silent killer of productivity. When people don't feel supported, when they feel like they have to be "on" all the time, they start checking out, mentally and emotionally. The work suffers. The morale tanks. The results go downhill.

You might think you're doing the right thing by being a workhorse, but if you're pushing your team too hard, you're creating an environment where people don't feel valued. You're teaching them that their well-being doesn't matter. That their family, their personal time, their mental health—none of that matters.

And guess what happens when people feel like they're nothing more than cogs in the machine? They stop caring. They do the bare minimum. They start looking for jobs elsewhere. You'll be left with a team that's exhausted, disengaged, and actively searching for an escape.

HOW TO BREAK FREE FROM the Insomniac Trap

Step one: Understand that hard work doesn't mean constant work. It's time to embrace the concept of balance. Leading by example doesn't mean showing up at 6 a.m. and leaving at midnight. It means knowing when to step back, rest, and recharge so you can perform at your best. It means being strategic with your time, not just filling it with endless tasks. Show your team that it's okay to take a break, to disconnect, and to have a life outside of work.

Step two: Set clear expectations and boundaries. Stop creating a culture where overworking is the norm. If you're responding to emails in the middle of the night, your team will feel obligated to do the same. Set the example by creating boundaries—and respect them. Show your team that it's okay to step away from work, that they can put their phones down and enjoy their personal time without guilt. When you give your

THE 12 LEADERSHIP TRAPS: WHICH ONE ARE YOU STUCK IN?

team permission to disconnect, you give them permission to be more productive and engaged when they are at work.

Step three: Delegate like a leader. You're not a superhero. You don't have to do everything yourself. Trust your team. Delegate tasks, empower people to take ownership, and stop trying to do everything on your own. A real leader knows when to step back and let others step up. That's how you build a strong, motivated, and engaged team.

Step four: Rest and recharge. You can't lead if you're running on empty. Rest is crucial to maintaining productivity, creativity, and focus. It's time to practice what you preach—take care of yourself. Get the sleep you need. Disconnect. Spend time with your family. Take a walk. Read a book. Whatever it takes to recharge your batteries. When you do this, you'll return to work with a clearer mind, more energy, and the ability to make better decisions.

FINAL THOUGHTS

If you're an Insomniac, it's time to get real. Working nonstop is not a badge of honor—it's a recipe for burnout and disengagement. The best leaders know that success comes not from endless hours at the desk, but from creating a sustainable, balanced environment where the team can thrive. It's time to put your workaholism aside, set some boundaries, and show your team that it's okay to step back and recharge. Because in the end, a well-rested, engaged team is the one that gets results—not the one that's running on empty.

Chapter 12: The Diva

Ah, the Diva. The center of attention. The one who believes that everything revolves around them. They make everything about their personal drama, need constant validation, and always want to be the star of the show. It doesn't matter what the actual problem is—they'll somehow find a way to make it about them. The Diva leader isn't about the team. They're about themselves. And, if you're the one stuck with a Diva at the helm, you already know how exhausting that is.

Let's get one thing straight: being a leader doesn't mean the world owes you anything. You're not the boss because you're some sort of royalty—you're there to guide, inspire, and drive your team toward success. But the Diva leader doesn't get that. They think leadership is all about being adored, receiving endless compliments, and having everyone bow down to their brilliance. They want the spotlight on them all the time, regardless of the situation. The bigger the ego, the more likely it is they'll overshadow the team's accomplishments, undermining everything the group works hard for.

THE PROBLEM WITH THE Diva

If you're the Diva, you'll often find yourself surrounded by yes-men or people who are afraid to speak up because they know they'll face some sort of backlash if they don't comply. These people will go along with everything you say, even if they know it's a terrible idea, because they're too intimidated to challenge your opinion. And let's face it—nobody likes a boss who uses their position as a power trip.

THE 12 LEADERSHIP TRAPS: WHICH ONE ARE YOU STUCK IN?

The Diva leader doesn't really care about the team. It's all about their own glory, their own accolades, and their own self-worth. If you're not boosting their ego, you're not useful to them. If you dare to challenge their views, they'll throw a tantrum or dismiss you entirely. The result? A toxic environment where team morale is non-existent, communication is stifled, and the team's true potential never sees the light of day. A team full of fear, frustration, and disengagement—sounds like a nightmare, doesn't it?

Instead of celebrating the team's successes, the Diva makes sure they're the one at the front of every victory parade, taking all the credit, basking in the glory. When something goes wrong? Well, that's the team's fault, isn't it? The Diva isn't going to take the blame. They'll throw anyone under the bus if it means protecting their precious image. So, instead of cultivating a high-performing, cohesive team, you get a group of people who don't trust their leader and are disengaged because they see their hard work going unrecognized. That's not leadership. That's a recipe for resentment.

THE IMPACT ON YOUR Team

The Diva's toxic attitude doesn't just impact their own personal credibility. It has a massive ripple effect on the entire team. When a leader operates from a place of ego, people begin to disengage. The focus shifts from team success to individual glory. Ideas are shut down because the Diva needs to be the one with the best idea. Contributions from the team are ignored because they don't serve the Diva's agenda. Team members are left feeling invisible, undervalued, and demotivated.

You might think you're "empowering" your team, but really, you're creating an environment where people are afraid to speak up. The Diva's leadership style breeds fear, and fear kills innovation and creativity. When people feel like they're just background noise to the Diva's grand performance, they stop trying. They stop caring. They stop speaking up.

And before long, all you have left is a team of passive followers who are too intimidated to share their thoughts or even contribute to the success of the company.

The worst part? The Diva doesn't even realize how much damage they're causing. They think their charisma, their charm, and their larger-than-life personality are enough to keep everyone motivated. But what they fail to understand is that leadership is about more than just showing up in style. It's about creating an environment where people feel valued. It's about recognizing your team's contributions. It's about giving credit where credit is due, even if it means you're not the one getting all the accolades.

HOW TO BREAK FREE FROM the Diva Trap

If you've been in the Diva trap for too long, here's some hard truth: it's time to check your ego at the door. Leadership isn't about you. It's about your team. A leader's success is measured by the success of their people, not by how many pats on the back they get. So, how do you stop acting like a Diva? Here's what you need to do:

Step one: Recognize that you're not the center of the universe. It's hard, I know. But get over yourself. Leadership isn't about constantly being in the spotlight. It's about guiding, motivating, and recognizing the efforts of your team. Start focusing on what they bring to the table. When you make it about them, you make them want to work harder. They'll respect you for it.

Step two: Give credit where credit is due. When your team hits a milestone, give them the recognition they deserve. Don't steal their thunder just to make yourself look good. Leaders lift others up, not step on them to climb higher. Be the person who celebrates your team's victories and acknowledges their hard work. It's time to share the glory.

Step three: Stop taking all the credit. The Diva might love the spotlight, but guess what? It's time to share it. When a project succeeds, remind everyone that it was a team effort. That means you were only successful because of the work your team put in. Your job as a leader is to foster success—not to bask in it alone. It's time to stop treating everything like your personal win.

Step four: Start being vulnerable. A true leader isn't afraid to admit their mistakes. They don't need to maintain a perfect image. They can show their team that they're human too. If you've made a mistake, own it. If you need help, ask for it. Vulnerability breeds trust. And when your team trusts you, they'll work for you—not because they're afraid, but because they believe in you.

FINAL THOUGHTS

If you're stuck in the Diva trap, it's time to do some serious self-reflection. Leadership is not about making it all about you. It's about empowering your team to succeed and putting their needs ahead of your own ego. Stop playing the role of the drama queen and start being the kind of leader who creates space for others to shine. When you learn to give credit, share the spotlight, and support your team, you'll realize that true leadership is about lifting others up, not just lifting yourself.

Conclusion: Breaking Free from the 12 Leadership Traps

Let's recap. By now, you've taken a brutally honest look at yourself through the 12 leadership traps. You've confronted the Control Freak who can't let go, the Ghost Boss who hides from responsibility, and the Cheerleader who's all rah-rah without the hard feedback. You've seen the Volcano, erupting at the smallest provocation, and the Visionary who's full of grand ideas but lacks follow-through. The Spreadsheet Overlord has likely made an appearance, hoarding data while ignoring the humans doing the work. The Social Butterfly? Well, maybe it's time to ditch the office politics and focus on leadership. And let's not forget about the Rulebook, clinging to outdated policies that stifle creativity and progress.

The Idea Tornado, the Zen Master, the Insomniac, and the Diva—they all show up in their own special ways. Each one of these traps has one thing in common: they limit your effectiveness as a leader. They hold you back, and, more importantly, they hold your team back.

Now, you're at a crossroads. The traps are in front of you, staring you down like a bad habit you can't shake. But here's the thing: you have the power to change. You can take action. You can get out of these traps and become the leader your team deserves. You don't need to be perfect, but you do need to be committed to progress. That's where the real work begins.

Let's break down the 12 traps again in case you need a quick reminder of where to start. The Control Freak needs to trust their team. The Ghost Boss needs to show up and engage. The Cheerleader has to learn when to give constructive feedback, not just empty praise. The Volcano needs to learn how to control their temper and remain steady in the face of stress. The Visionary has to stop talking about ideas and start executing. The Spreadsheet Overlord needs to recognize that data is just one piece of the puzzle, not the whole story. The Social Butterfly should focus on results, not just personal popularity. The Rulebook needs to relax its grip on rigid policies and embrace flexibility. The Idea Tornado needs to finish what they start. The Zen Master should get a little more fired up when it counts. The Insomniac needs to realize that their pace isn't sustainable, and neither is expecting the same from their team. Finally, The Diva must put their ego aside and focus on the team, not their own spotlight.

The first step to breaking free from these traps is recognizing them in the first place. Congratulations—you've already done that. Now, it's time to act.

This isn't going to be easy. Change never is. But the good news is that you don't have to do it alone. You can seek feedback, get a coach (shameless plug: like me), and lean on the resources available to you. You can change, but only if you're willing to put in the work. No one is going to hand you a magic formula. If you want to stop being the Control Freak, you'll need to learn how to let go. If you want to stop being the Ghost Boss, you'll need to engage and be present. If you want to stop being the Diva, well, your ego has to take a backseat.

Leadership isn't about being perfect. It's about being real, being honest, and being willing to grow. So, what's next? Start small. Take one trap you're caught in and focus on it. Don't try to fix everything at once—it's a recipe for burnout. Focus on one action item for each trap, and take a deliberate step every day to break free. Whether it's trusting your team more, having those tough conversations, or learning to manage your temper, the key is to take consistent action. It's about progress, not perfection.

Also, remember that breaking free from these traps isn't a one-time event. It's an ongoing process. Every day is an opportunity to make a new choice. You'll slip up. You'll revert to old habits. But that's okay—just recognize it and get back on track. Leadership is a marathon, not a sprint. But with each small step, you'll move further away from the traps and closer to becoming the kind of leader you know you can be.

So here's your final call to action: identify the trap or traps you're most stuck in. Be brutally honest with yourself. Ask for feedback from those around you—your team, your peers, your boss. Then, take action. One step at a time. Every day. You don't need a roadmap to success. You just need the courage to take the first step. And the second. And the third. You get the idea.

The world doesn't need more leaders who are stuck in their own traps. The world needs leaders who are willing to face their weaknesses, tackle their flaws, and continuously improve. That's how you'll not only break free from the traps but become the kind of leader who inspires others to do the same. So go ahead—take that first step. Your team—and your future self—will thank you.

About the Author

Marako Marcus is a consultant, coach, and public speaker with a reputation for being straight to the point—no fluff, no excuses. He helps executives, teams, and individuals face their challenges head-on, cutting through the corporate nonsense and delivering results that matter. With years of experience working with organizations of all sizes, Marako knows exactly what's wrong with most workplaces and how to fix them—without the usual corporate jargon.

A master of tough love and tough conversations, he's a coach who tells it like it is and makes sure you know exactly where you stand. His approach is simple: if you're not getting it done, stop whining and start acting. He's worked with leaders who need a wake-up call and teams who need someone to light a fire under them.

When he's not stirring up success in the business world, Marako unleashes his creativity as a musician. Yes, he's the guy who can juggle spreadsheets and compose a killer track at the same time—proving that sharp focus can strike the right chord in both the boardroom and the studio. Marako's blend of directness and creativity makes him a unique voice in the business world—and someone you'll want to listen to.

BOOK LINKS AVAILABLE at https://linktr.ee/marakomarcusbooks

www.ingramcontent.com/pod-product-compliance
Lightning Source LLC
Chambersburg PA
CBHW070413230526
45471CB00006B/2781